MOVIE POSTERS

volume eighteen of
the illustrated history of movies through posters

Images from the Hershenson-Allen Archive

Previous Volumes:
Volume One: Cartoon Movie Posters
Volume Two: Cowboy Movie Posters
Volume Three: Academy Award® Winners' Movie Posters
Volume Four: Sports Movie Posters
Volume Five: Crime Movie Posters
Volume Six: More Cowboy Movie Posters
Volume Seven: Horror Movie Posters
Volume Eight: Best Pictures' Movie Posters
Volume Nine: Musical Movie Posters
Volume Ten: Serial Movie Posters
Volume Eleven: Horror, Sci-Fi & Fantasy Movie Posters
Volume Twelve: Comedy Movie Posters
Volume Thirteen: War Movie Posters
Volume Fourteen: Attack of the "B" Movie Posters
Volume Fifteen: Not Nominated Movie Posters
Volume Sixteen: To Be Continued… 1930's & 1940's Serial Movie Posters
Volume Seventeen: Who Goes There?… 1950's Horror & Sci-Fi Movie Posters

Edited by Richard Allen and Bruce Hershenson
Published by Bruce Hershenson
P.O. Box 874, West Plains, MO 65775
Phone: (417) 256-9616 Fax: (417) 257-6948
mail@brucehershenson.com (e-mail)
http://www.brucehershenson.com or
http://www.emovieposter.com (website)

IF YOU ENJOYED THIS MOVIE POSTER BOOK, THEN YOU ARE SURE TO ENJOY THESE OTHER SIMILAR BRUCE HERSHENSON PUBLICATIONS. LOOK FOR THEM AT YOUR LOCAL BOOKSTORE OR ORDER THEM DIRECT FROM THE PUBLISHER.

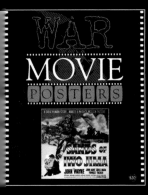

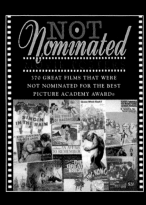

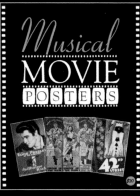

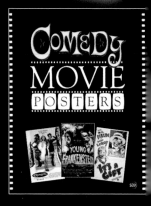

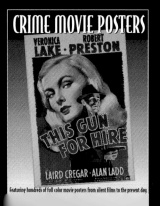

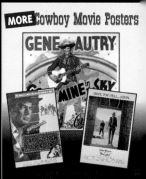

INTRODUCTION

Welcome to the eighteenth volume of the Illustrated History of Movies Through Posters. This book is intended to serve as a companion volume to the fourteenth book of this series, Attack of the "B" Movie Posters, which included posters from some of the worst films ever made (but with wild and outrageous poster art and taglines that promised far more than the films delivered). That volume had a greater emphasis on horror and science fiction posters than does this volume. **Note that this volume has NO duplications from Attack of the "B" Movie Posters.**

This volume is entitled "Drive-In Movie Posters" because I believe most moviegoers immediately think of a certain type of film when they hear the words, "drive-in movie", and the films represented in this volume all fall into that genre. I cannot state for a fact that all of these films were actually shown at drive-in movie theaters, although they would certainly not be out of place in that setting!

Where did the images in this book come from? They are contained within the archive I co-own with my partner, Richard Allen, the Hershenson-Allen Archive. The archive consists of over 35,000 different movie poster images, all photographed directly from the original posters onto high quality 4" x 5" color transparencies. There is not another resource like it anywhere, and it is the world's foremost source of movie poster images. The Archive has provided images for books, videos, DVDs, magazines, and newspapers

Unless otherwise noted, the image in this volume is of the original U.S. one-sheet poster (the standard movie poster size, measuring 27" x 41"), from the first release of the film. There are also lobby cards, which measure 11" x 14". Lobby cards were normally produced in sets of eight, with one card that often had artwork and credits, called a Title Card, and seven scene lobby cards that show actual scenes from the film (colorized if the film was made in black and white).

This is not a catalog of posters for sale, nor do I sell any sort of movie poster reproductions! However, I do sell movie posters of all sorts through auctions, primarily over the Internet, and in the past 12 years I have sold over 16 million dollars of movie paper! If you are interested in acquiring original vintage movie posters (or any of the other 30 books I have published) visit my website at http://www.brucehershenson.com (the most visited vintage movie poster site on the Internet with over 425,000 visitors to date) or send a self-addressed stamped envelope to the address on the title page for free brochures.

I need to thank Amy Knight who did the layouts and designed the covers for this book, and Courier Graphics, who printed it. Most of all, I need to thank my partner, Richard Allen. He has always loved movie posters of all years and genres, and he helped track down the images in this book. We share a common vision, and we hope to keep publishing these volumes until we have covered every possible genre of film.

I dedicate this book to one of the first and greatest collectors (and dealers) of movie posters and lobby cards, Marty Davis, formerly of Ohio, but recently re-located to West Granby, Ct. Marty has a love of movie paper that covers all eras and genres, although his first love is the films of Buster Keaton and Charlie Chaplin. From the first day I met Marty twelve years ago (when we talked so long about posters that he was late for his wedding rehearsal!), he has always been willing to share his extensive knowledge of movie paper with me, and he has allowed me to reproduce many rare items from his collection in this series of books. I thank him for all he has done for me, but most of all, I am glad to have him as my friend!

Bruce Hershenson

January 2002

1. FLAMING YOUTH, 1923, lobby card

2. BARE KNEES, 1928, lobby card

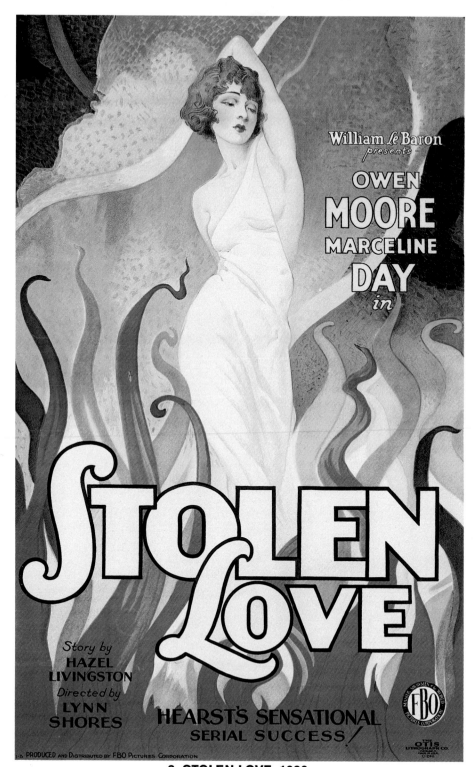

3. STOLEN LOVE, 1928

4. TRADER HORN, 1931, lobby card

5. UNDER EIGHTEEN, 1931, Title lobby card

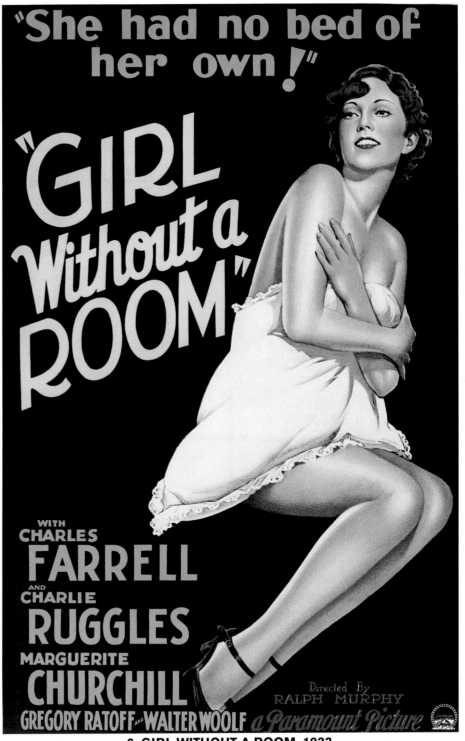

6. GIRL WITHOUT A ROOM, 1933

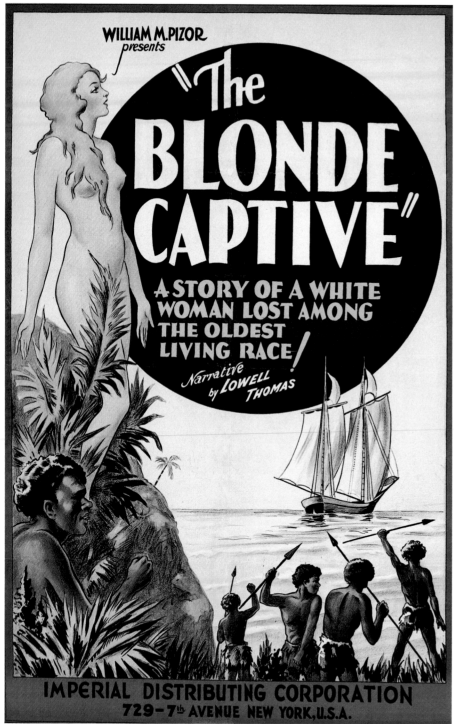

7. THE BLONDE CAPTIVE, 1937

8. SLAVES IN BONDAGE, 1937

9. CHILD BRIDE, 1938

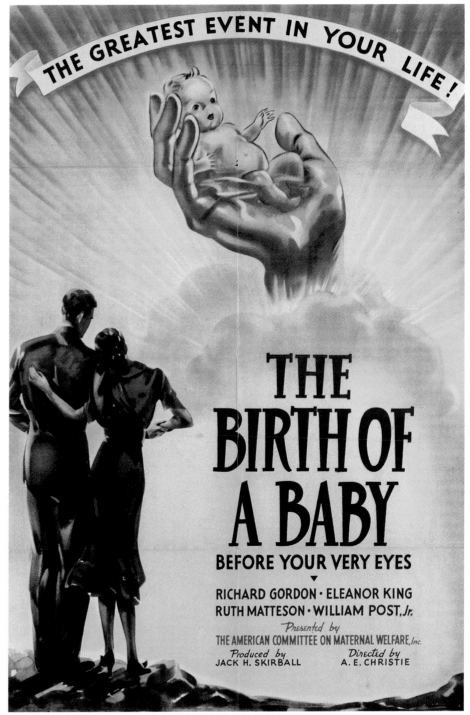

10. THE BIRTH OF A BABY, 1938

11. ESCORT GIRL, 1941

12. HITLER'S CHILDREN, 1942, lobby card

13. JUKE GIRL, 1942, Title lobby card

14. CONFESSIONS OF A VICE BARON, 1942

15. WHITE PONGO, 1945, Title lobby card

16. THE WHITE GORILLA, 1945, lobby card

17. T-MEN, 1947, lobby card

18. THE CURSE OF THE UBANGI, 1947, Title lobby card

19. BECAUSE OF EVE, 1948

26. THEY LIVE BY NIGHT, 1949, lobby card

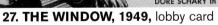
27. THE WINDOW, 1949, lobby card

28. HOLLYWOOD BURLESQUE, 1949

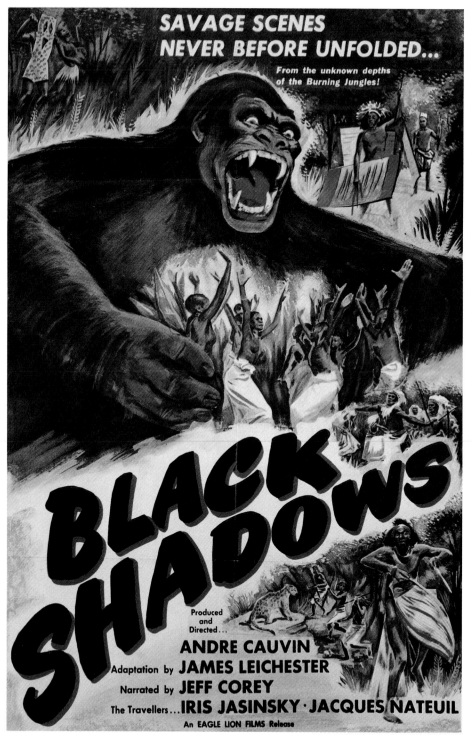

29. BLACK SHADOWS, 1949

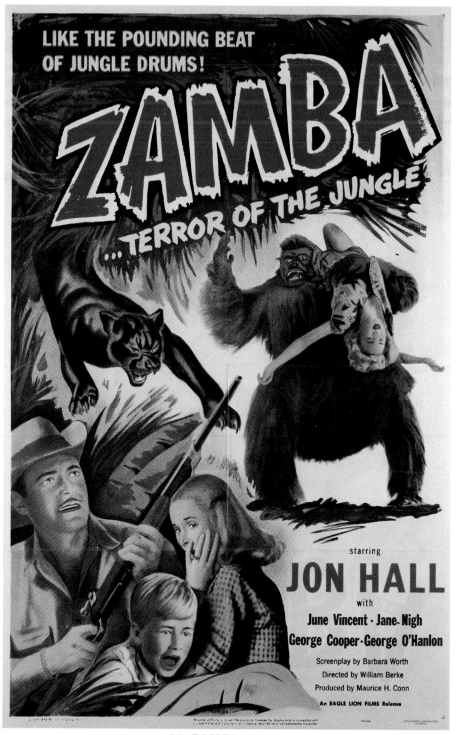

30. ZAMBA, 1949

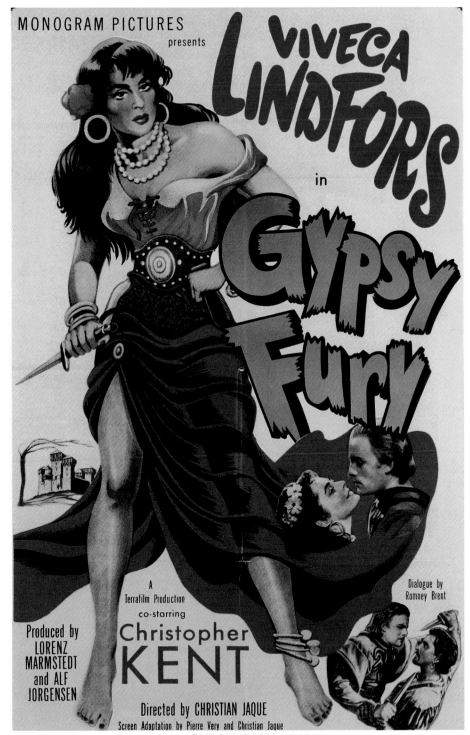

31. GYPSY FURY, 1949

32. THE DALTONS' WOMEN, 1950

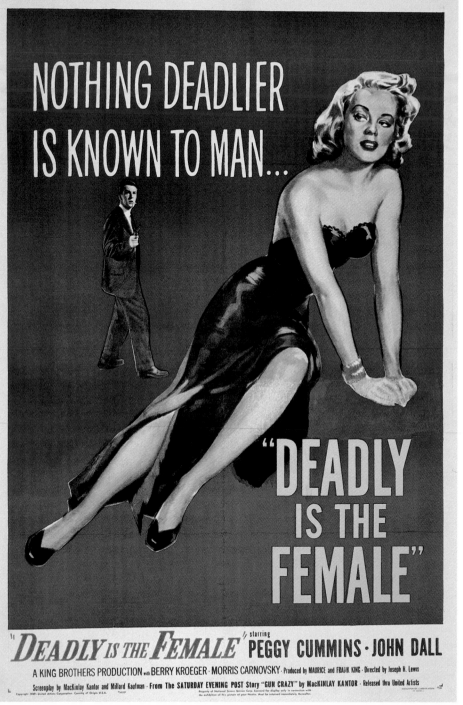

33. DEADLY IS THE FEMALE (GUN CRAZY), 1950

34. A MODERN MARRIAGE, 1950

35. PREHISTORIC WOMEN, 1950, lobby card

36. DARK CITY, 1950, lobby card

37. NATIVE SON, 1950

38. TRY AND GET ME, 1950

39. TRY AND GET ME, 1950

40. THE DEVIL'S SLEEP, 1951

TODAY'S MORAL MENACE!..

DARING EXPOSE OF THE DEVIL DRUG · TRAFFIC IN 'BENNIES' · 'GOOFIES' and 'PHENOS' AS IT REALLY EXISTS

"The DEVIL'S SLEEP"

With a Brilliant Cast Starring

LITA GREY CHAPLIN
JOHN MITCHUM
WILLIAM THOMASON
TRACY LYNNE

and introducing

GEORGE EIFERMAN

(MR. AMERICA)

TIMOTHY FARRELL

and a BEVY OF GORGEOUS HOLLYWOOD STARLETS

A SCREEN CLASSICS PRODUCTION

PRODUCED BY GEORGE WEISS

DIRECTED BY W. MERLE CONNELL

41. TWO-DOLLAR BETTOR, 1951

DON'T BE A SUCKER!

THE TRUE STORY OF A NICE GUY "TAKEN" -BUT GOOD!

I BET!

I STOLE!

I WON!

I KILLED!

I LOST!

I PAID!

$2. WIN

JACK BRODER PRODUCTIONS PRESENTS "TWO-DOLLAR BETTOR"

STARRING JOHN LITEL · MARIE WINDSOR · STEVE BRODIE

Produced and Directed by EDWARD L. CAHN

JACK BRODER PRODUCTION

42. MAN BAIT, 1952

43. STRANGE FASCINATION, 1952

44. KID MONK BARONI, 1952

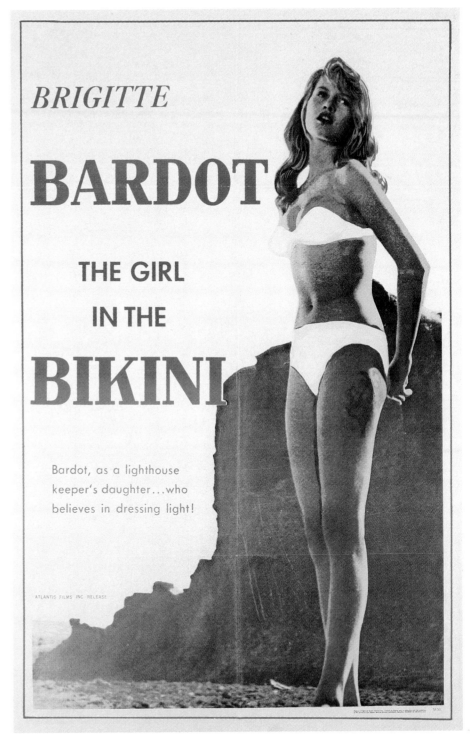

45. THE GIRL IN THE BIKINI, 1952, released in the U.S. in 1958

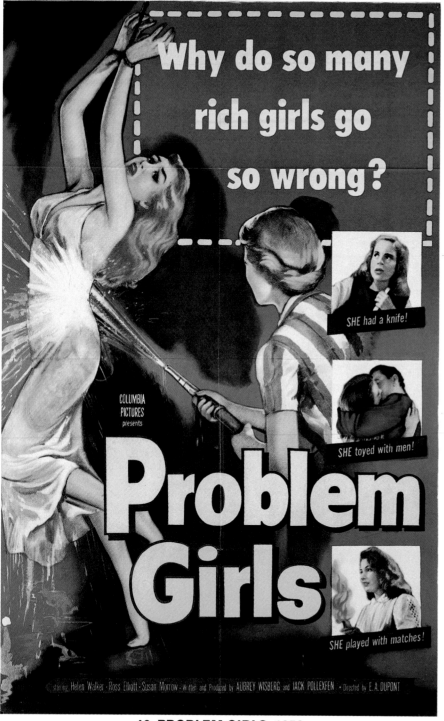

46. PROBLEM GIRLS, 1953

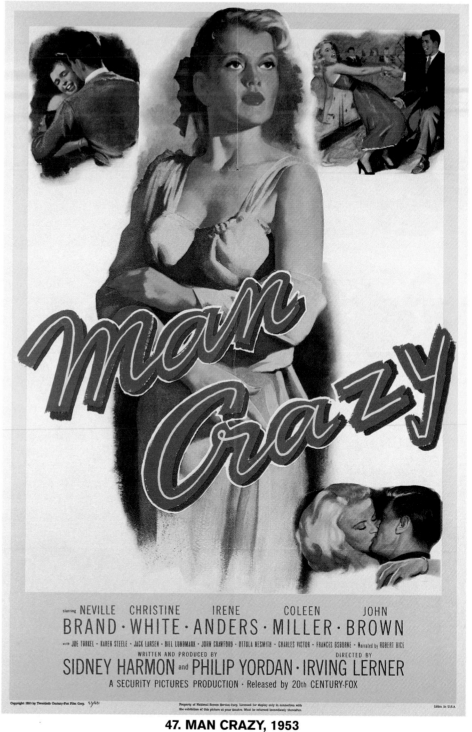

47. MAN CRAZY, 1953

48. THE FRENCH LINE, 1954

49. UNDERWATER, 1955

50. TEENAGE CRIME WAVE, 1955, lobby card

51. MADEMOISELLE STRIPTEASE, 1956, lobby card

52. HOT CARS, 1956

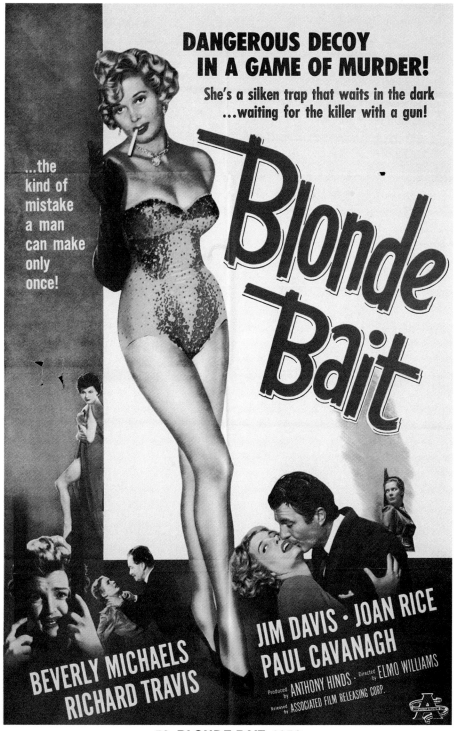

53. BLONDE BAIT, 1956

54. BLONDE SINNER, 1956

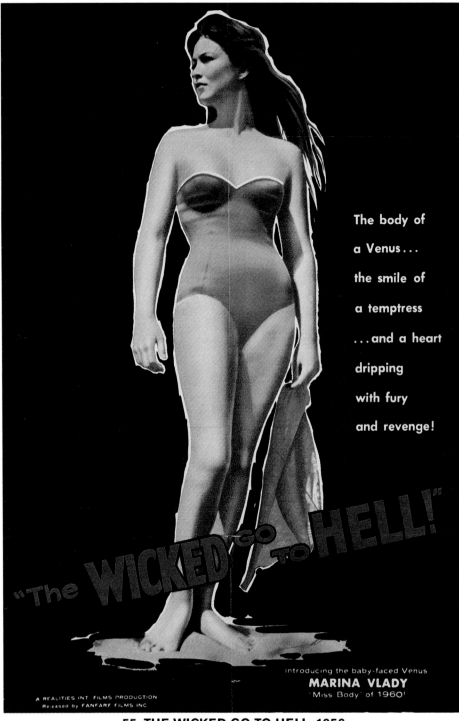

The body of
a Venus...
the smile of
a temptress
...and a heart
dripping
with fury
and revenge!

"The WICKED GO TO HELL!"

introducing the baby-faced Venus
MARINA VLADY
"Miss Body" of 1960!

A REALITIES INT FILMS PRODUCTION
Released by FANFARF FILMS INC

55. THE WICKED GO TO HELL, 1956

They called her "JAILBAIT"!

RUNAWAY DAUGHTERS

starring
MARLA ENGLISH · ANNA STEN · JOHN LITEL · LANCE FULLER · ADELE JERGENS

co-starring
Mary Ellen KAYE and Gloria CASTILLO · A GOLDEN STATE PRODUCTION · Produced by ALEX GORDON
Directed by EDWARD L. CAHN · Executive Producer: SAMUEL Z. ARKOFF · Story and Screenplay: LOU RUSOFF · An AMERICAN-INTERNATIONAL Picture

56. RUNAWAY DAUGHTERS, 1956

57. THE BLACK SLEEP, 1956

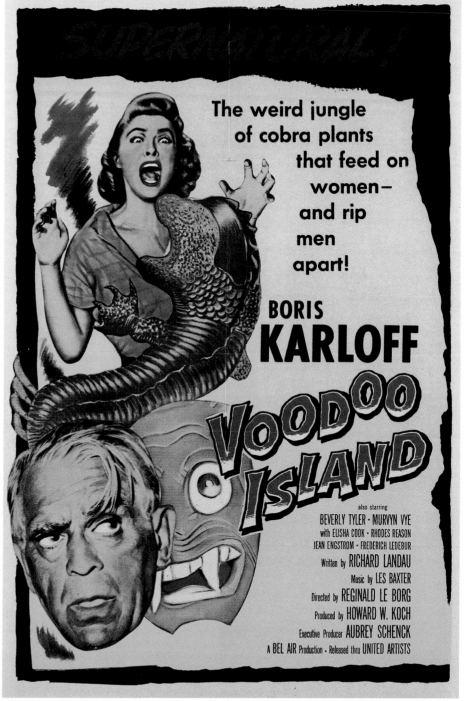

58. VOODOO ISLAND, 1957

59. THE INCREDIBLE SHRINKING MAN, 1957, lobby card

60. FROM HELL IT CAME, 1957, lobby card

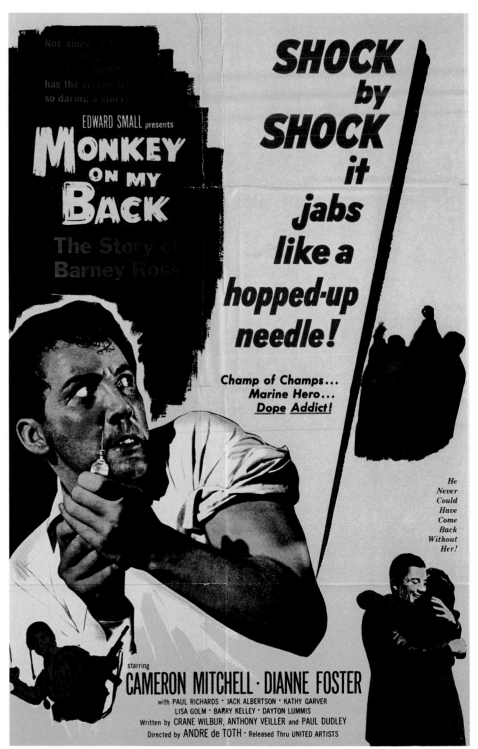

61. MONKEY ON MY BACK, 1957

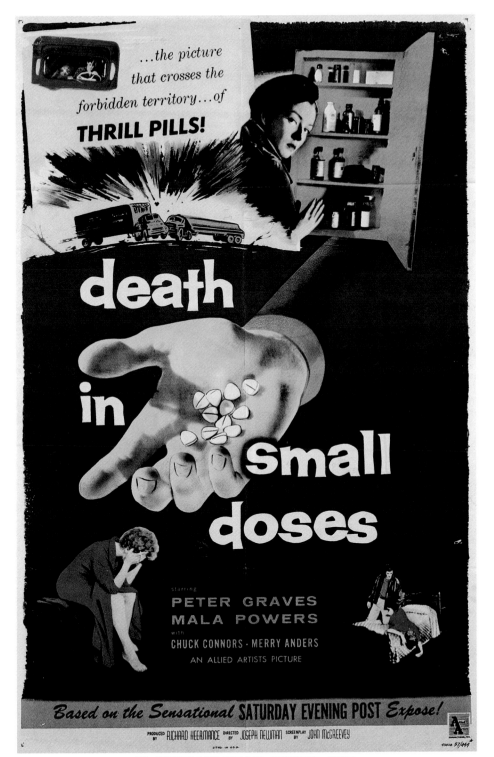

62. DEATH IN SMALL DOSES, 1957

63. THE AMAZING COLOSSAL MAN, 1957, lobby card

64. BEGINNING OF THE END, 1957, lobby card

65. THE UNHOLY WIFE, 1957

66. NAKED IN THE SUN, 1957

67. HIT AND RUN, 1957

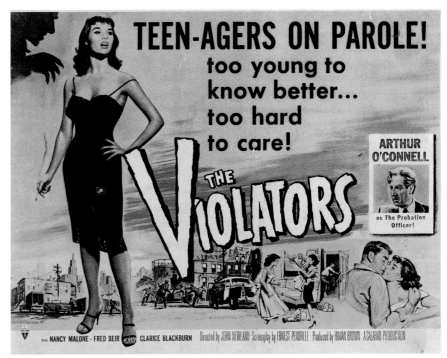

68. THE VIOLATORS, 1957, Title lobby card

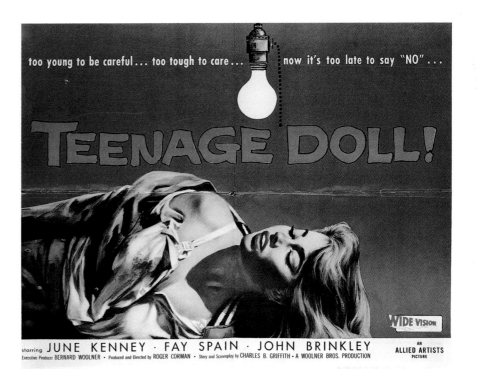

69. TEENAGE DOLL, 1957, half-sheet

70. **HOW TO MAKE A MONSTER, 1958,** lobby card

71. **THE BRIDE AND THE BEAST, 1958,** lobby card

72. **UNWED MOTHER, 1958**

73. JUVENILE JUNGLE, 1958

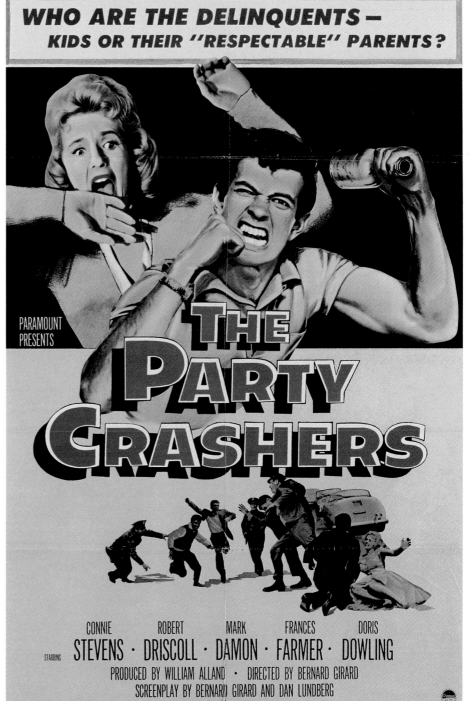

74. THE PARTY CRASHERS, 1958

75. THE INCREDIBLE PETRIFIED WORLD, 1959

76. THE DAY THE EARTH FROZE, 1959

77. BORN TO BE LOVED, 1959

78. THE GIRL IN LOVERS' LANE, 1959

WANTED!

52460	84255	99202	82443	32725
BIG PEARL — Armed Robbery, Stage Holdups, Homicide (Three counts), Jailbreaking.	**FARO KITTY** — Common Gambler, Possessor of Firearms, Homicide.	**CRAZY HANNAH** — Strangler, Subject to fits of temporary Homicidal Insanity.	**MISSOURI LADY** — (Wife of Missouri Kid) — Possession of Firearms, Harboring Known Killer, Assault with Intent to Kill.	**MARIA "THE KNIFE"** — Manslaughter, allegedly in defense of her honor.

They Used A Weapon No Badman Could...SEX!

GLENN H. McCARTHY presents

Five Bold Women

A JIM ROSS FILM PRODUCTION

They Killed <u>BOLD</u>!
They Robbed <u>BOLD</u>!
They Loved <u>BOLD</u>!

in EASTMAN COLOR

starring JEFF MORROW · MERRY ANDERS · JIM ROSS featuring GUINN "BIG BOY" WILLIAMS · IRISH McCALLA · KATHY MARLOWE

with LUCITA BLAIN · DEE CARROLL · ROBERT CAFFEY · GEORGE KRAMER · directed by JORGE LOPEZ-PORTILLO · story — screenplay by MORTIMER BRAUS and JACK POLLEXFEN · A CITATION FILMS RELEASE

79. FIVE BOLD WOMEN, 1959

T-BIRD GANG

THE ONE YEAR OUT OF HIGH SCHOOL CROWD— FAST CARS, GIRLS... NO PLACE TO GO!

80. T-BIRD GANG, 1959, lobby card

SHE WALKS by NIGHT

WOOLNER BROS. present

starring BELINDA LEE

Screen Play by JOACHIM BARTSCH · DIETER FRITKO · Produced by RUDOLF JUGERT · A RAPID FILM · UNION FILM Release

81. SHE WALKS BY NIGHT, 1959, lobby card

82. THE PUSHER, 1960

83. BEAT GIRL, 1960

84. TORMENTED, 1960, lobby card

85. GORGO, 1960, lobby card

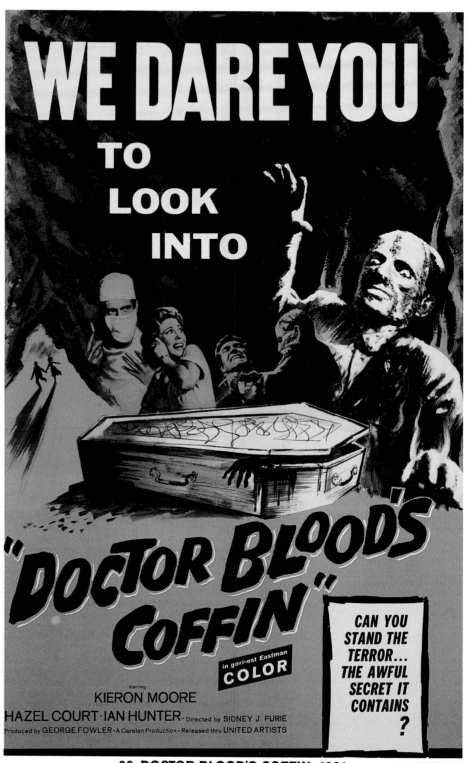

86. DOCTOR BLOOD'S COFFIN, 1961

87. THE SNAKE WOMAN, 1961

88. TWIST ALL NIGHT, 1961

89. WOMEN OF NAZI GERMANY, 1962

90. THE MAN WHO FINALLY DIED, 1962

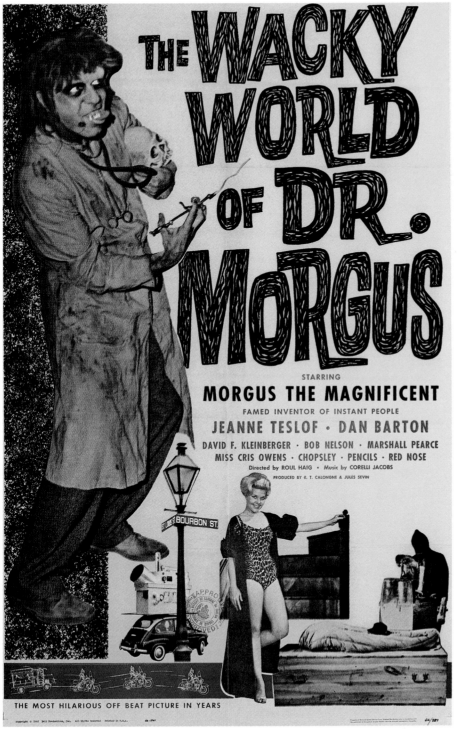

91. THE WACKY WORLD OF DR. MORGUS, 1962

92. THE CREATION OF THE HUMANOIDS, 1962

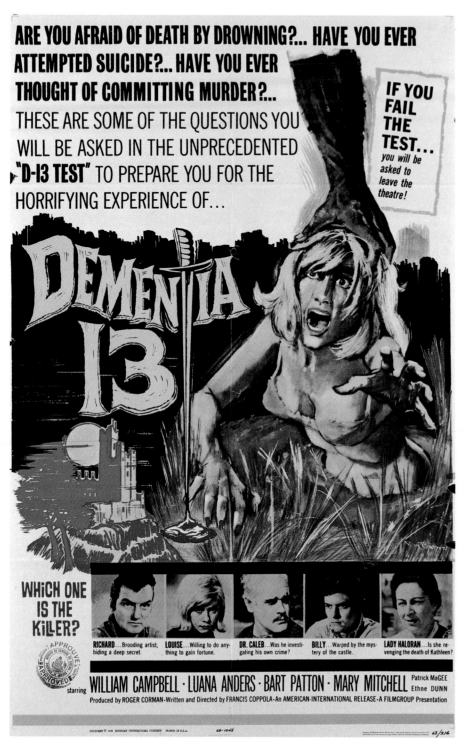

93. DEMENTIA 13, 1963

94. THE MOLESTERS, 1963

95. THE STRANGLER, 1964

96. BUNNY YEAGER'S NUDE CAMERA, 1964, lobby card

97. THE NAKED KISS, 1964, lobby card

98. MUDHONEY, 1965

99. ROPE OF FLESH (MUDHONEY), 1965

100. HORRORS OF SPIDER ISLAND, 1965

101. THE GHOST AND MR. CHICKEN, 1965

102. TEENAGE MOTHER, 1966

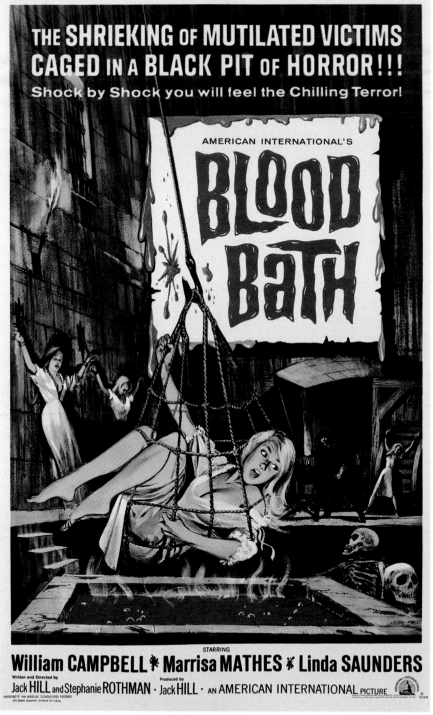

103. BLOOD BATH, 1966

104. BLOOD FIEND, 1967

105. HILLBILLYS IN A HAUNTED HOUSE, 1967

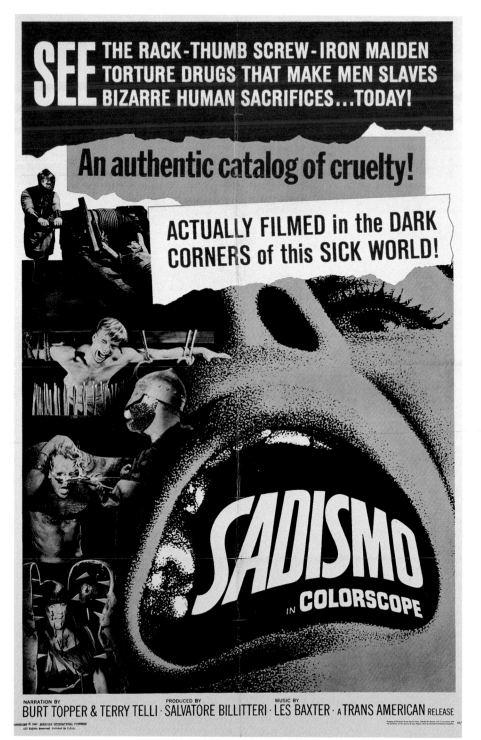

106. SADISMO, 1967

107. SPREE, 1967

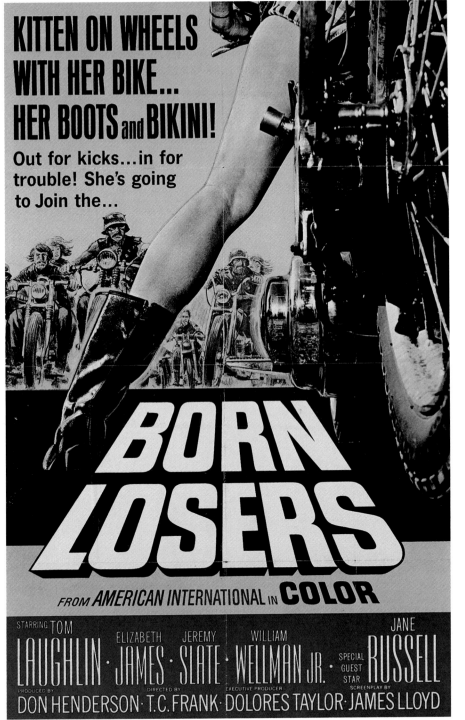

108. BORN LOSERS, 1967

109. THE HELLCATS, 1967

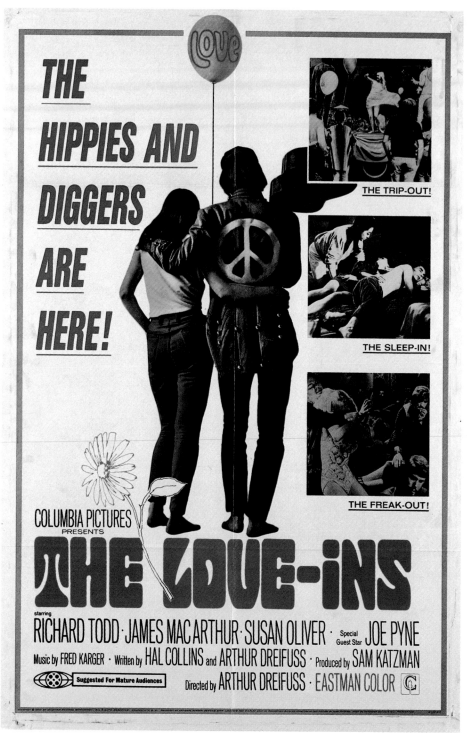

110. THE LOVE-INS, 1967

111. THE TRIP, 1967

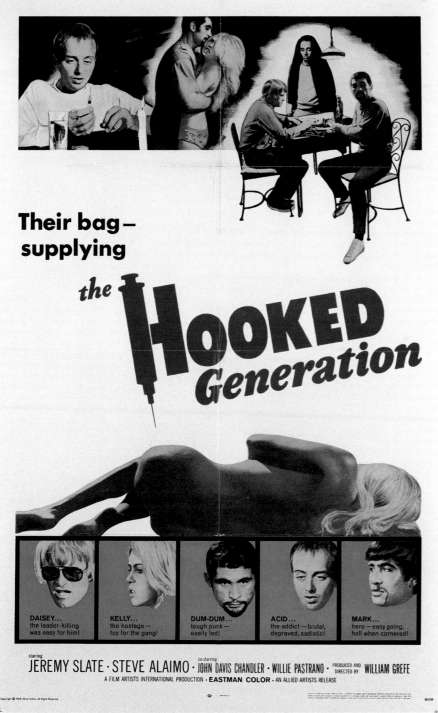

112. THE HOOKED GENERATION, 1967

113. MARYJANE, 1968

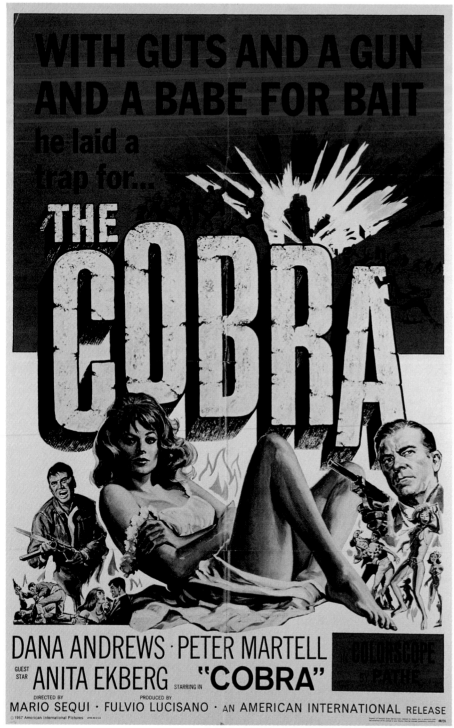

114. THE COBRA, 1968

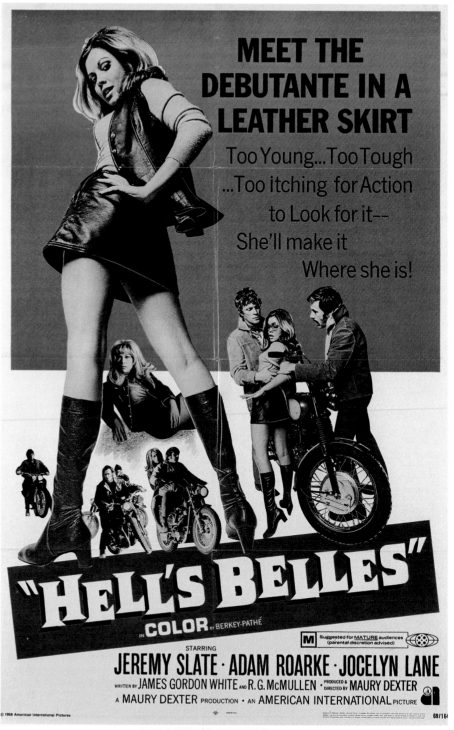

115. HELL'S BELLES, 1968

116. SATAN'S SADISTS, 1969

117. THE CHRISTINE JORGENSEN STORY, 1970

118. FLESH FEAST, 1970

119. THE HITCHHIKERS, 1971

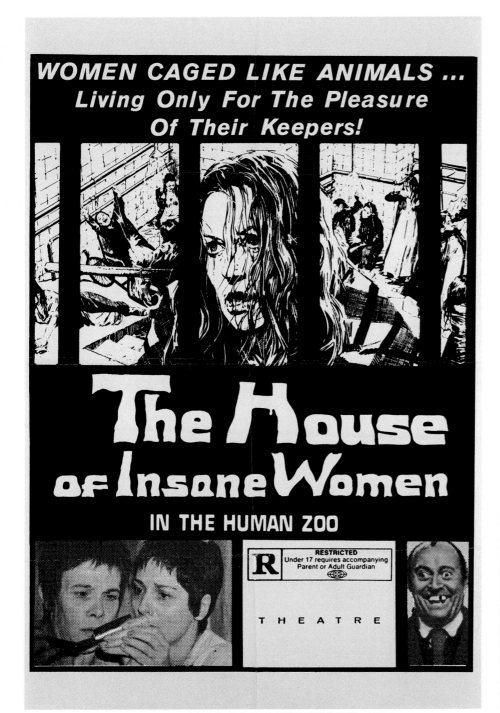

120. THE HOUSE OF INSANE WOMEN, 1971

121. THE INCREDIBLE 2 HEADED TRANSPLANT, 1971

122. WEREWOLVES ON WHEELS, 1971

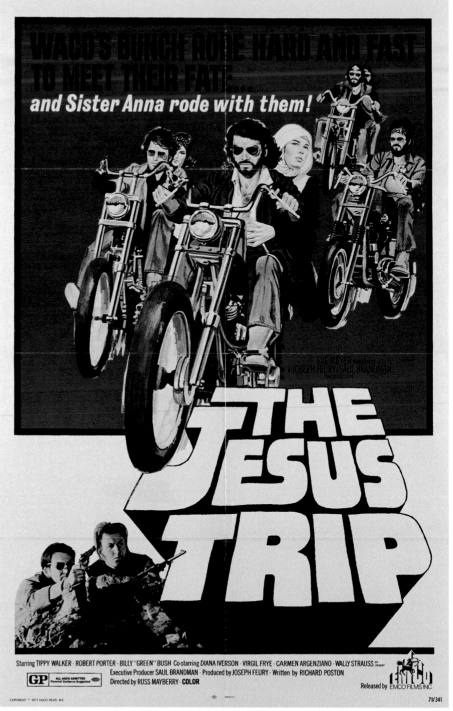

123. THE JESUS TRIP, 1971

124. POT! PARENTS! POLICE!, 1971

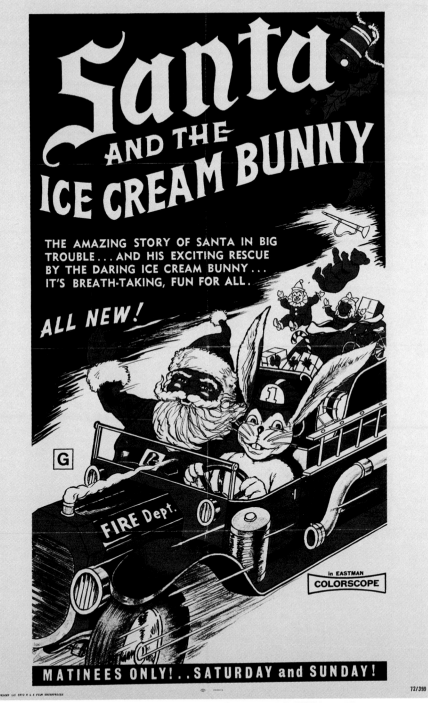

125. SANTA AND THE ICE CREAM BUNNY, 1972

126. PICK UP ON 101, 1972

127. I WANT WHAT I WANT, 1972

128. SEDUCE AND DESTROY, 1973

129. SUPERCHICK, 1973

She's the "GODMOTHER" of them all

...The baddest One-Chick Hit-Squad that ever hit town!

R RESTRICTED
Under 17 Requires Accompanying Parent or Adult Guardian

"Coffy"

130. COFFY, 1973

She's "Ten miles of bad road" for every hood in town!

6 feet 2" and all of it Dynamite!

Cleopatra Jones

131. CLEOPATRA JONES, 1973

THE BLACK MOSES OF SOUL

ISAAC HAYES

special

TERRY LEVENE PRESENTS AN AQUARIUS FILMS RELEASE OF A CHUCK JOHNSON PRODUCTION PRODUCED AND DIRECTED BY CHUCK JOHNSON · COLOR

 GENERAL AUDIENCES
All Ages Admitted

Design by
Creative Cinema Campaigns

132. THE BLACK MOSES OF SOUL, 1973

ANDY WARHOL'S
YOUNG
Dracula
A FILM BY PAUL MORRISSEY

young Dracula has so much trouble with the opposite sex that he's carrying around his own stake looking for a guy with a hammer!

ANDY WARHOL'S "YOUNG DRACULA"
A FILM by PAUL MORRISSEY · Starring
Joe Dallesandro · Udo Kier · Victoria de Sica · Roman Polanski
A CARLO PONTI-ANDY WARHOL PRODUCTION · COLOR · A CENTRAL PARK FILMS RELEASE

133. ANDY WARHOL'S YOUNG DRACULA, 1974

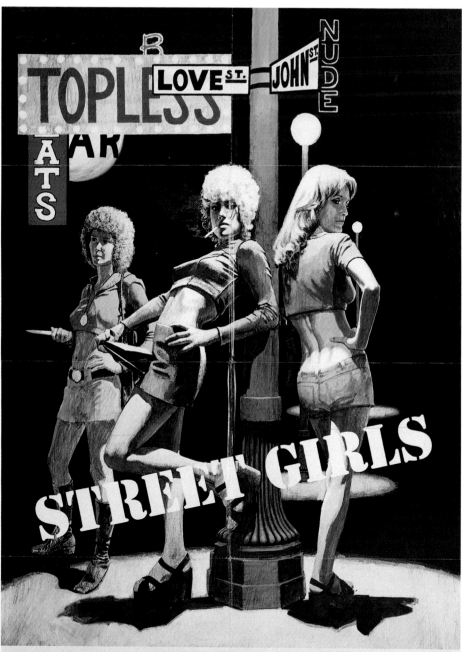

134. STREET GIRLS, 1974

135. THE BLACK GESTAPO, 1975

136. 'GATOR BAIT, 1976

137. SCORCHY, 1976

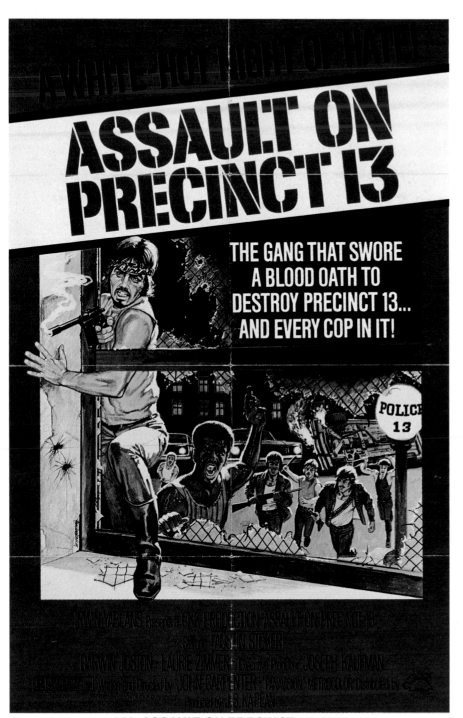

138. ASSAULT ON PRECINCT 13, 1976

139. SCHIZO, 1977

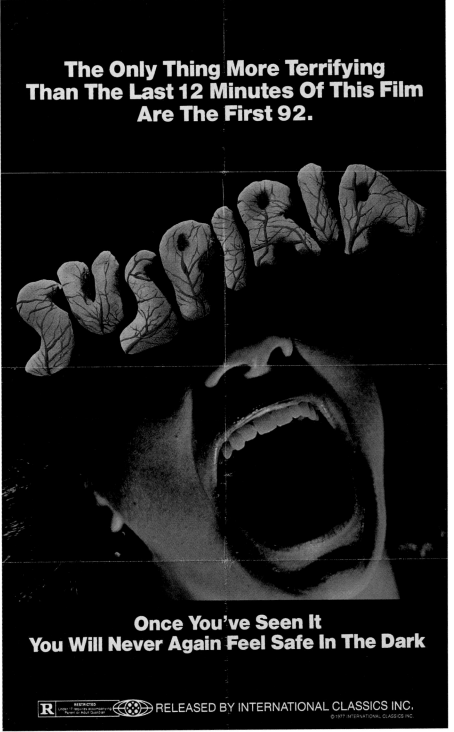

140. SUSPIRIA, 1977

141. FINGERS, 1978

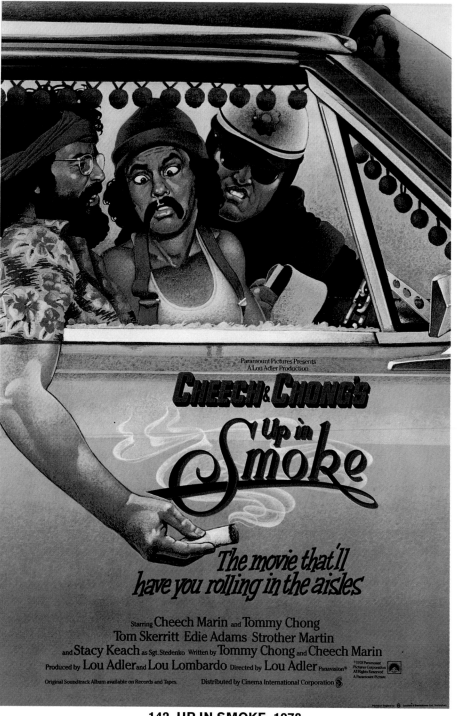

142. UP IN SMOKE, 1978

143. I SPIT ON YOUR GRAVE, 1978

144. KIDNAPPED COED, 1978

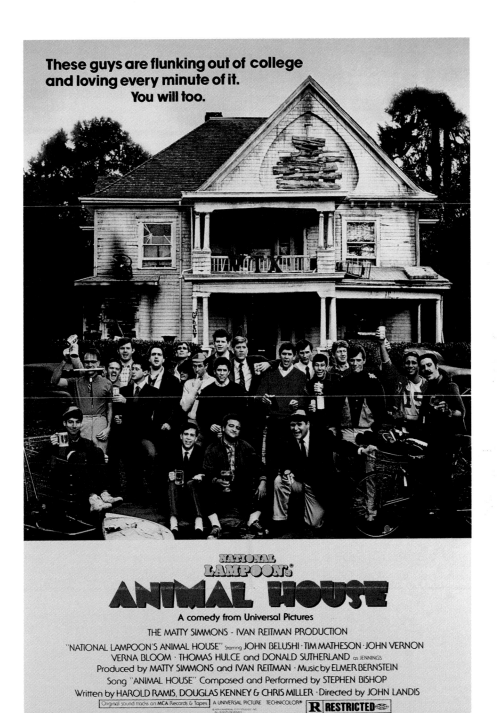

145. NATIONAL LAMPOON'S ANIMAL HOUSE, 1978

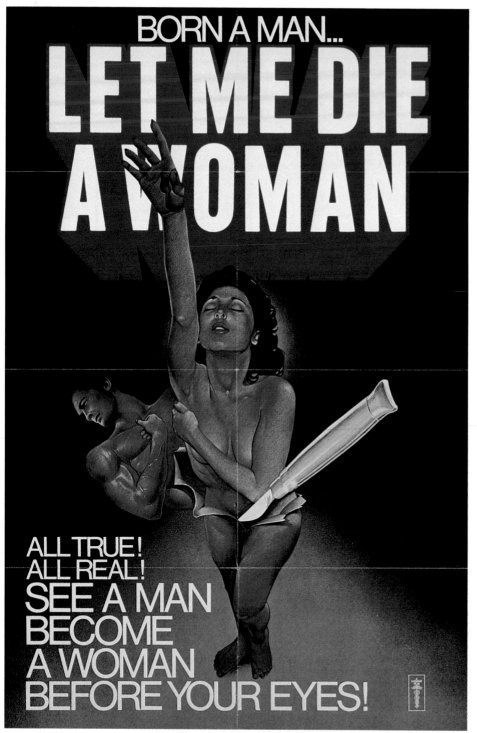

146. LET ME DIE A WOMAN, 1978

147. MALIBU BEACH, 1978

148. BARRACUDA, 1978

149. MONSTER, 1979

150. UP FROM THE DEPTHS, 1979

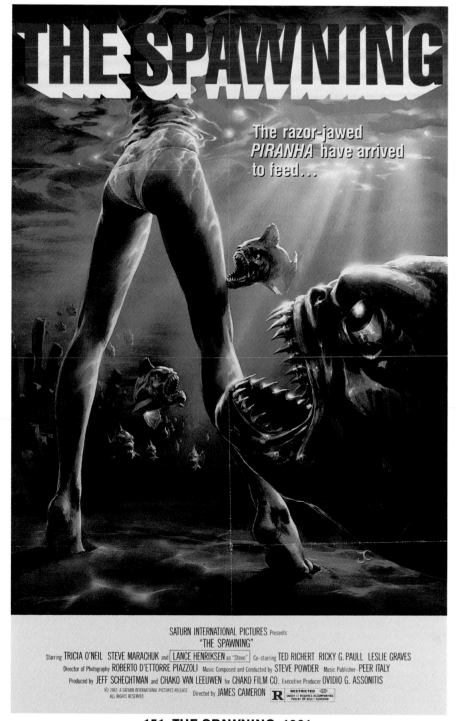

151. THE SPAWNING, 1981

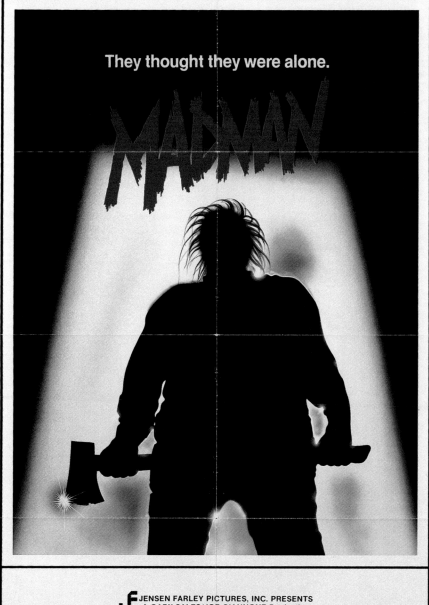

They thought they were alone.

MADMAN

152. MADMAN, 1981

A SHOCKING FILM!

The image of a generation

At 12
it was Angel Dust.

At 13
it was heroin.

Then she took
to the streets.

With **DAVID BOWIE**

Christiane F.

153. CHRISTIANE F., 1981

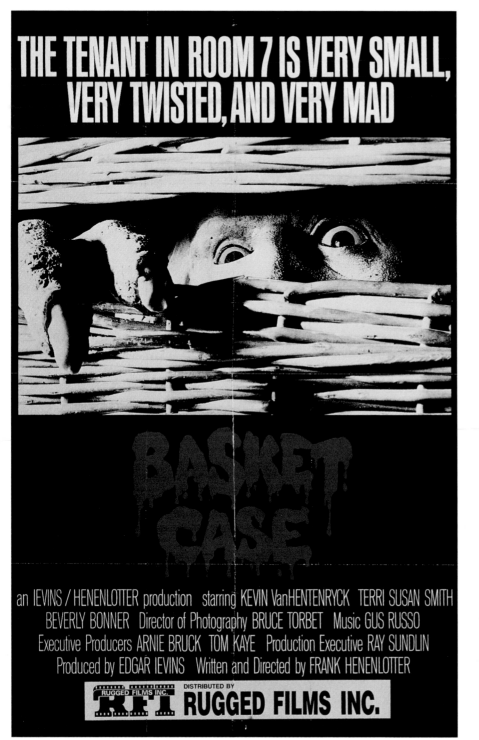

154. BASKET CASE, 1982

155. EYE OF THE EVIL DEAD, 1982

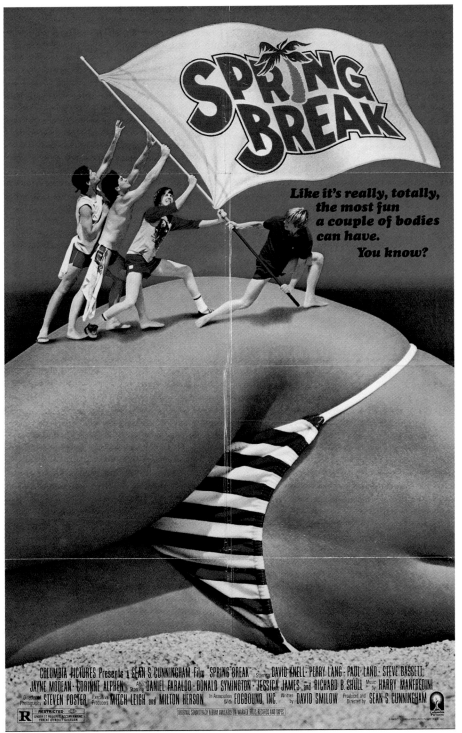

156. SPRING BREAK, 1983

157. VALLEY GIRL, 1983

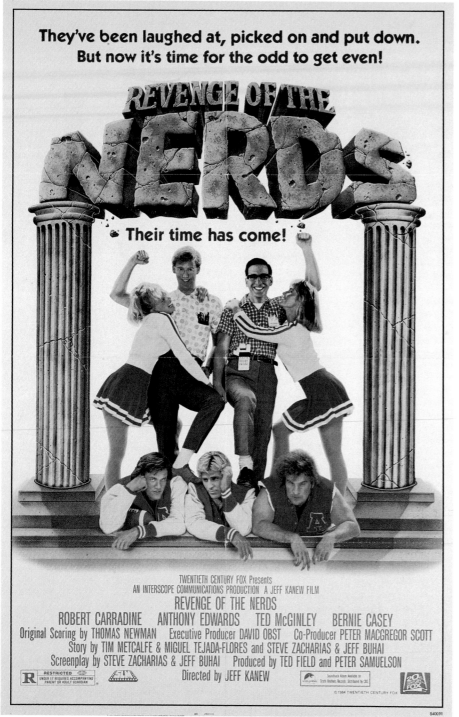

158. REVENGE OF THE NERDS, 1984

159. REPO MAN, 1984

NO MAN CAN TOUCH HER NAKED STEEL.

BARBARIAN QUEEN

BORIS ©85

Starring LANA CLARKSON · KATT SHEA · FRANK ZAGARINO · DAWN DUNLAP
Produced by FRANK ISAAC and ALEX SESSA   Screenplay by HOWARD R. COHEN
Directed by HECTOR OLIVERA

160. BARBARIAN QUEEN, 1985

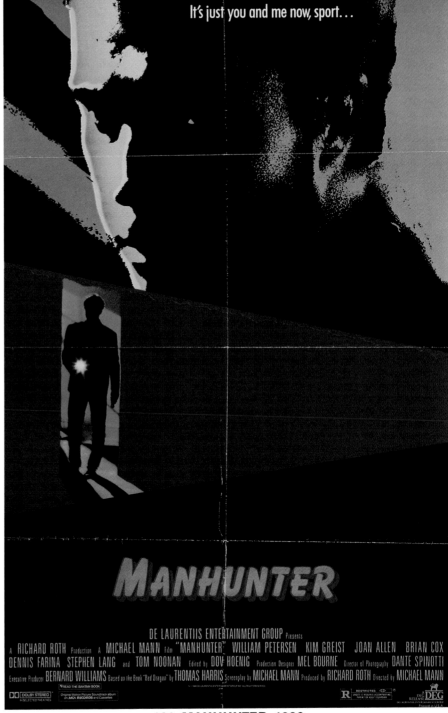

It's just you and me now, sport...

MANHUNTER

DE LAURENTIIS ENTERTAINMENT GROUP Presents

A RICHARD ROTH Production A MICHAEL MANN film "MANHUNTER" WILLIAM PETERSEN KIM GREIST JOAN ALLEN BRIAN COX
DENNIS FARINA STEPHEN LANG and TOM NOONAN Edited by DOV HOENIG Production Designer MEL BOURNE Director of Photography DANTE SPINOTTI
Executive Producer BERNARD WILLIAMS Based on the Book "Red Dragon" by THOMAS HARRIS Screenplay by MICHAEL MANN Produced by RICHARD ROTH Directed by MICHAEL MANN

161. MANHUNTER, 1986

162. CHOPPING MALL, 1986

163. CHOPPING MALL, 1986, video one-sheet

164. THE NEST, 1988

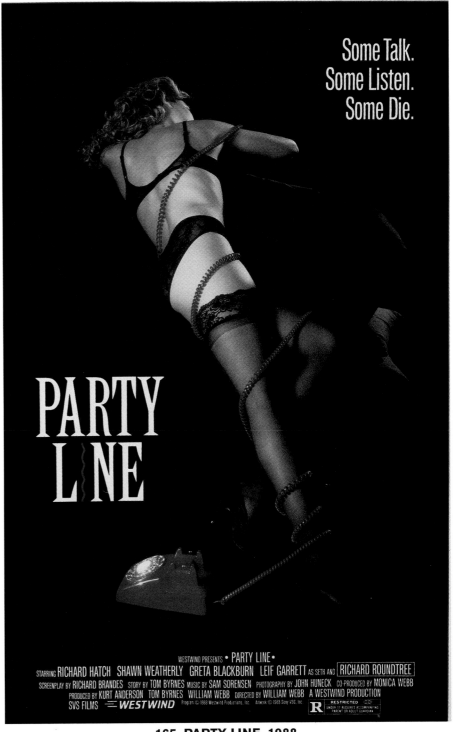

165. PARTY LINE, 1988

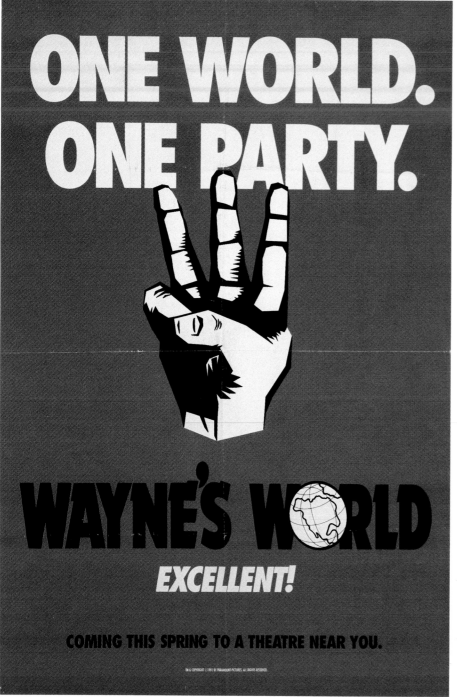

166. WAYNE'S WORLD, 1992

167. CLASS ACT, 1992

168. SCREAM, 1996

169. SCARY MOVIE, 2000

Drive-In
MOVIE POSTERS
INDEX